DELANEY
STREET
PRESS

The Gift of Friendship

The Gift of Friendship

A Treasury of Quotations
About Friends

By Criswell Freeman

DELANEY STREET PRESS
Nashville, TN
(800) 256-8584

ISBN 1-58334-063-7

The ideas expressed in this book are not, in all cases, exact quotations, as some have been edited for clarity and brevity. In all cases, the author has attempted to maintain the speaker's original intent. In some cases, material for this book was obtained from secondary sources, primarily print media. While every effort was made to ensure the accuracy of these sources, the accuracy cannot be guaranteed. For additions, deletions, corrections or clarifications in future editions of this text, please write DELANEY STREET PRESS.

Printed in the United States of America
Cover Design by Bart Dawson
Typesetting & Page Layout by Sue Gerdes

1 2 3 4 5 6 7 8 9 10 • 00 01 02 03 04 05 06

ACKNOWLEDGMENTS

The author gratefully acknowledges the helpful support of Angela Beasley Freeman, Dick and Mary Freeman, Mary Susan Freeman, Jim Gallery, and supportive professionals at WALNUT GROVE PRESS and DELANEY STREET PRESS.

*For Lisa and the
Entire Elcan Family*

Table of Contents

Each friend represents
a world in us, a world
possibly not born until
they arrive, and it is
only by this meeting
that a new world
is born.

Anaïs Nin

1

The Gift of Friendship

Ralph Waldo Emerson once observed, "A friend may well be reckoned the masterpiece of nature." Emerson understood that a genuine friend is a treasure beyond price. On the pages that follow, we consider that timeless treasure, the crowning glory of a well-lived life: the gift of friendship.

The real friend is another self.

Cicero

The better part of one's life consists
of his friendships.

Abraham Lincoln

Friendship is a single soul dwelling
in two bodies.

Aristotle

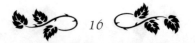

A friend is a present
you give yourself.

Robert Louis Stevenson

Friendship is the source of the greatest pleasures, and without friends even the most agreeable pursuits become tedious.

Saint Thomas Aquinas

I keep my friends as misers do their treasure, because, of all things granted us by wisdom, none is greater or better than friendship.

Pietro Aretino

Friendship is the only cement that will ever hold the world together.

Woodrow Wilson

We are all travelers
in the desert of life, and
the best we can find
on our journey is
an honest friend.

Robert Louis Stevenson

Strangers are what friends are made of.
Cullen Hightower

Since there is nothing so well worth
having as friends, never lose a chance
to make them.
Francesco Guicciardini

The making of friends who are real
friends is the best token we have
of a man's success in life.
Edward E. Hale

The best time to make friends
is before you need them.
Ethel Barrymore

There is no wilderness like a life
without friends.
Baltasar Gracián

Robbing life of friendship is like
robbing the world of the sun.
Cicero

The most beautiful discovery true friends
make is that they can grow separately
without growing apart.
Elizabeth Foley

Other people are like a mirror
which reflects back on us the kind
of image we cast.
Bishop Fulton J. Sheen

To be capable of steady friendship
or lasting love are the two greatest proofs,
not only of goodness of heart, but of
strength of mind.
William Hazlitt

Think where man's glory most begins
and ends, And say my glory was
I had such friends.

W. B. Yeats

A faithful friend is the medicine of life.

Old Proverb

A man cannot be said to succeed in
this life who does not satisfy one friend.

Henry David Thoreau

A true friend is
forever a friend.

George Macdonald

The companions of our childhood always
possess a certain power over our minds.
Mary Wollstonecraft Shelley

There's no friend like someone who
has known you since you were five.
Anne Stevenson

Friendship takes time.

Agnes Repplier

Friendship is not quick to burn.

May Sarton

Real friendship is a slow grower.

Lord Chesterfield

It is great to have friends when we are young, but indeed it is still more so when we are getting old. When we are young, friends are, like everything else, a matter of course. In the old days, we know what it means to have them.

Edvard Grieg

One friend in a
lifetime is much;
two are many; three
are hardly possible.

Henry Adams

As in the case of wines that improve with age, the oldest friendships ought to be the most delightful.

Cicero

Old friends are the great blessing of one's later years. They have a memory of the same events and have the same mode of thinking.

Horace Walpole

Wherever you are, it is your friends who make your world.

William James

Friends are an aid to the young,
to guard them from error; to the elderly,
to attend to their wants; to those
in the prime of life, to assist them
to noble deeds.

Aristotle

If you want an accounting of your worth,
count your friends.

Merry Browne

Without friends no one would choose
to live, though he had all other goods.

Aristotle

I have learned that to
have a good friend is the
purest of all God's gifts,
for it is a love that
has no exchange
of payment.

Frances Farmer

2

The Gift of Kindness

Kindness is the foundation of a lasting friendship. As Sophocles observed, "One who knows how to show and to accept kindness will be a friend better than any possession."

On the pages that follow, we consider ways that considerate deeds and compassionate words build friendships — and change lives.

He who sows courtesy
reaps friendship, and he
who plants kindness
gathers love.

Saint Basil

Scatter seeds of kindness.

George Ade

Goodness is the only investment
that never fails.
Henry David Thoreau

The important things are to have
genuine interest in people and to be kind
to them. Kindness, I've discovered,
is everything in life.
Isaac Bashevis Singer

I am quite sure that no friendship yields
its true pleasure and nobility of nature
without frequent communication,
sympathy and service.
George E. Woodberry

Many a friendship — long, loyal, and self-sacrificing — rested at first upon no thicker a foundation than a kind word.
Frederick W. Faber

Life is an exciting business and most exciting when lived for other people.
Helen Keller

None is so near the gods as he who shows kindness.

Seneca

Kind words can be
short and easy to speak,
but their echoes are
truly endless.

Mother Teresa

There is no love which does not
become help.

Paul Tillich

Kindness is the language which
the deaf can hear and the blind can see.

Mark Twain

The best portion of a good man's life is
his little, nameless, unremembered acts
of kindness and of love.

William Wordsworth

No act of kindness,
no matter how small,
is ever wasted.

Aesop

3

The Gift of Trust

Over 2000 years ago, the Roman philosopher Cicero observed, "Loyalty is what we seek in friendship." Nothing has changed since then. Loyalty is still the gold standard by which we measure our most valuable friendships. In this chapter, wise men and women consider the worth of a trustworthy friend and arrive at a single conclusion: The gift of trust is priceless.

I can trust my friends.
These people force me
to examine myself, and
they encourage me
to grow.

Cher

The best mirror is a trusted, old friend.

Sephardic Saying

The shifts of fortune test the reliability of friends.

Cicero

The firmest friendships have been formed in mutual adversity, as iron is most strongly united by the fiercest flame.

Charles Caleb Colton

Friendship, of itself a holy tie, is made more sacred by adversity.

John Dryden

In prosperity our
friends know us;
in adversity we know
our friends.

John Churton Collins

No man can be happy without a friend
nor be sure of his friend
till he is unhappy.

Thomas Fuller

Real friendship is shown in times
of trouble; prosperity is full of friends.

Euripides

The friend of my adversity I shall always
cherish most.

Ulysses S. Grant

Good friends are
like shock absorbers.
They help you take
the lumps and bumps
on the road of life.

Frank Tyger

She is a friend.
She gathers the pieces and gives them
back to me in all the right order.

Toni Morrison

Friends — real friends —
reserve nothing.

Euripides

Confidence is the foundation
of friendship. If we give it,
we will receive it.

Harry E. Humphreys, Jr.

My friend is he who will tell me
my faults, in private.
Ibn Gabirol

A friend can tell you things you
don't want to tell yourself.
Frances Ward Weller

Friendship, by its very nature, is freer
of deceit than any other relationship.
Francine du Plessix Gray

A good friend who points out mistakes
and imperfections and rebukes evil
is to be respected as if he reveals
a secret of hidden treasure.

Buddha

A doubtful friend is worse than a
certain enemy. Let a man be one or the
other, and then we know how to meet him.

Aesop

A friend to everybody and nobody
is the same thing.

Spanish Proverb

A faithful friend is a strong defense;
and he that hath found such a one
hath found a treasure.

Ecclesiasticus 6:14

Trouble is a sieve through which we sift
our acquaintances. Those too big to pass
through are our friends.

Arlene Francis

When a friend is in trouble, don't annoy him by asking if there is anything you can do. Think up something appropriate and do it.

Edgar Watson Howe

Actions, not words,
are the true criteria
of the attachment
of friends.

George Washington

The real friend is he
or she who can share
all our sorrow and
double our joys.

B. C. Forbes

4

The Gift of Happiness

Happiness is a natural byproduct of friendship. As Joseph Addison writes, "Friendship improves happiness and abates misery by doubling our joy and dividing our grief." On the pages that follow, thoughtful men and women consider ways that good friends make life tolerable in times of trouble and joyful in times of triumph.

Of all the things
that wisdom provides
to make life happy,
by far the greatest
is friendship.

Epicurus

Friends are the sunshine of life.

John Hay

Lead the life that will make you kindly
and friendly to everyone about you, and
you will be surprised what a happy life
you will live.

Charles M. Schwab

Happiness to me is enjoying my friends
and family.

Reba McEntire

Years and years of happiness only make us realize how lucky we are to have friends who have shared and made that happiness a reality.

Robert E. Frederick

Good friends, good books and a sleepy conscience: This is the ideal life.

Mark Twain

Happiness is a habit. Cultivate it.

Elbert Hubbard

A cheerful friend is
like a sunny day which
spreads its brightness
on all around.

John Lubbock

Happiness always looks small while
you hold it in your hands, but let it go,
and you learn at once how big
and precious it is.

Maxim Gorky

When we recall the past, we usually
find that it is the simplest things — not
the great occasions — that in retrospect
give off the greatest glow of happiness.

Bob Hope

Happiness grows at our own firesides
and is not to be picked in
strangers' gardens.

Douglas Jerrold

Ah, how good
it feels! The hand
of an old friend.

Henry Wadsworth Longfellow

Happiness is a matter of one's most
ordinary everyday mode of consciousness:
being busy and lively and
unconcerned with self.

Iris Murdoch

Too many wish to be happy
before becoming wise.

Suzanne Curchod Necker

The foolish man seeks happiness in the
distance, the wise grows it under his feet.

J. Robert Oppenheimer

Joy is not in things, it is in us.
Richard Wagner

The worst solitude is to be destitute
of sincere friendship.
Francis Bacon

Friendship has splendors
that love knows not.
Mariama Bâ

Happiness is achieved only by making others happy.

Stuart Cloete

The happiest people are those who do the most for others.

Booker T. Washington

Joy is what happens to us when we allow ourselves to recognize how good things really are.

Marianne Williamson

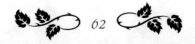

Shared joys make
a friend.

Friedrich Nietzsche

Happy is he to whom, in the maturer season of life, there remains one tried and constant friend.

Anna Letitia Barbauld

5

The Gift of Encouragement

From time to time, all of us need encouragement. Who better to provide that reassurance and support than a trusted friend? George Bernard Shaw writes, "The only service a friend can really render is to keep your courage up by holding up to you a mirror in which you can see a noble image of yourself." Encouraging friends remind us of the power within, and *therein* lies their value.

It takes a lot of
courage to show
your dreams to
someone else.

Erma Bombeck

True friends ... face in
the same direction
toward common
projects, interests
and goals.

C. S. Lewis

Just as despair can come only to one
from other human beings, hope, too,
can be given to one only
by other human beings.

Elie Wiesel

A friend should bear
his friend's infirmities.

William Shakespeare

To pull a friend out of the mire,
don't hesitate to get dirty.

Ba'al Shem Tov

Friendship is healing;
we are physicians
to each other.

Oliver Sacks

Friendship is the pleasing game
  of interchanging praise.
                Oliver Wendell Holmes, Sr.

Friendship is a strong and habitual
  inclination in two persons to promote
the good and happiness of one another.
                Eustace Budgell

No receipt opens the heart but a true
  friend, to whom you may impart griefs,
    joys, fears, hopes, suspicions,
      counsel, and whatever lies
        upon the heart.
                Francis Bacon

No one is useless in
the world who lightens
the burden of it
to anyone else.

Charles Dickens

It is not so much our friends' help that helps us, as the confidence of their help.

Epicurus

So long as we love we serve; so long as
we are loved by others, I would almost say
that we are indispensable; and no man
is useless while he has a friend.
Robert Louis Stevenson

But every road is tough to me that has
no friend to cheer it.
Elizabeth Shane

He who bears another
is borne by another.
St. Gregory the Great

A friend is one who
makes me do my best.

Oswald Chambers

He is our friend who loves us more
than admires us, and would aid us
in our great work.
William Ellery Channing

Friendship makes prosperity more brilliant
and lightens adversity by dividing and
sharing it.
Cicero

A sympathetic friend can be quite
as dear as a brother.
Homer

Tell a man he is brave and you help him become so.

Thomas Carlyle

Encouragement is the oxygen of the soul.

George M. Adams

The only way to have a friend
is to be one.
Ralph Waldo Emerson

Live for thy neighbor if thou wouldst
live for thyself.
Seneca

Be a friend to thyself,
and others will be so too.
Thomas Fuller

6

The Gift of Companionship

One of the most precious gifts we can share with a friend is time. When we take time to enjoy the presence of another person, and when we take care to understand that person, we demonstrate friendship in action. Physical presence is important to a friendship; emotional presence is essential. On the following pages, wise men and women remind us we don't get our best friends by accident; we earn them by sharing ourselves and our time.

True happiness arises from the enjoyment
of one's self and from the friendship and
conversation of a few select companions.
Joseph Addison

The most I can do for my friend is simply
to be his friend.
Henry David Thoreau

One thing everybody in the world wants
and needs is friendliness.
William E. Holler

Acquaintances ask about our outward
life; friends ask about our inner life.
Marie von Ebner-Eschenbach

We awaken in others the same attitude
of mind we hold toward them.
Elbert Hubbard

The balm of life — a kind and
faithful friend.
Mercy Otis Warren

Those who cannot give friendship
will rarely receive it and never hold it.
Dagobert D. Runes

Friendship with oneself is all-important,
because without it one cannot be friends
with anyone else in the world.
Eleanor Roosevelt

When good cheer is lacking,
our friends will be packing.
Unknown

Love is a mutual
self-giving which ends
in self-recovery.

Bishop Fulton J. Sheen

To make people into friends, listen to
them for hours at a time.
Rebecca West

If you want to be listened to, you should
put in time listening.
Marge Piercy

You can make more friends in two months
by becoming interested in other people
than you can in two years by trying to get
other people interested in you.
Dale Carnegie

The first duty of love
is to listen.

Paul Tillich

Keep the other person's well-being
in mind when you feel an attack
of soul-purging truth coming on.

Betty White

Don't flatter yourself that friendship
authorizes you to say disagreeable things
to your intimates. The nearer you come
into relation with a person, the more
necessary does tact and courtesy become.

Oliver Wendell Holmes, Sr.

It is wise to pour the oil of refined
politeness on the mechanism
of friendship.

Colette

When anger rises,
    think of the consequences.

Confucius

Politeness is an inexpensive way
    of making friends.

William Feather

Friendships, like marriages, are
    dependent on avoiding
    the unforgivable.

John D. MacDonald

'Tis the privilege of friendship to talk nonsense and have nonsense respected.
Charles Lamb

There is nothing we like to see so much as the gleam of pleasure in a person's eye when he feels that we have understood him.
Don Marquis

Silences make the real conversations between friends.
Margaret Lee Runbeck

Nothing in this world appeases loneliness
as does a flock of friends!
George Matthew Adams

Radiate friendship and it will return
sevenfold.
B. C. Forbes

Go oft to the house of thy friend,
for weeds choke the unused path.
Ralph Waldo Emerson

 *89*

There is only one thing better
than making a new friend, and that
is keeping an old one.
Elmer G. Leterman

The person who treasures friends
is solid gold.
Marjorie Holmes

Human beings are born into this little
span of life, and among the best things
that life has to offer are its friendships
and intimacies. Yet, humans leave their
friendships with no cultivation, letting
them grow as they will by the roadside.
William James

Friendship is a plant which must
be often watered.

Unknown

A man, sir, should keep his friendship
in constant repair.

Samuel Johnson

Hold a true friend with both hands.

African Proverb

When befriended, remember it.
When you befriend, forget it.
Poor Richard's Almanac

We should behave to our friends as we
would wish our friends to behave to us.
Aristotle

"Stay" is a charming word
in a friend's vocabulary.
Louisa May Alcott

We have really no absent friends.

Elizabeth Bowen

The influence of each
human being on others
in this life is a kind
of immortality.

John Quincy Adams

7

The Gift of Acceptance

The American philosopher William James once observed, "The art of being wise is knowing what to overlook." His words have special meaning for those who seek to establish long-lasting friendships. True friendships are built upon a spirit of acceptance, as the following quotations will attest.

Two persons cannot long be friends
if they cannot forgive each other's
little failings.

Jean de La Bruyère

True friends are the ones who really
know you but love you anyway.

Edna Buchanan

Who seeks a faultless friend
remains friendless.

Turkish Proverb

To be social is to be forgiving.

Robert Frost

To find a friend one must close one eye.
To keep him — two.

Norman Douglas

When my friends lack an eye,
I look at them in profile.

Joseph Joubert

It is one of the blessings of old friends
that you can afford to be stupid
with them.
Ralph Waldo Emerson

You can always tell a real friend:
When you've made a fool of yourself, he
doesn't feel you've done a permanent job.
Laurence J. Peter

A friend is a person who knows
all about you — and still likes you.
Elbert Hubbard

What I cannot love,
I overlook. That is
friendship.

Anaïs Nin

My friends have made the story of my
life. In a thousand ways they have turned
my limitations into beautiful privileges
and enabled me to walk serene and happy
in the shadow cast by my deprivation.
Helen Keller

The goodness, beauty and perfection
of a human being belongs to the one who
knows how to recognize these qualities.
Georgette Leblanc

Friendship flourishes at the fountain
of forgiveness.
William Arthur Ward

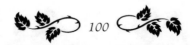

The essence of true friendship
is to make allowances for one another's
little lapses.

David Storey

Every man should have a fair-sized
cemetery in which to bury the faults
of his friends.

Henry Ward Beecher

My best friend is the man who
in wishing me well wishes it for my sake.

Aristotle

A friend is one who
sees through you and
still enjoys the view.

Wilma Askinas

8

The Gift of Love

Friendship, at its best, becomes a special kind of love. Friends, especially those with years of shared history, come to care deeply for each other. We conclude with words of wisdom about the love that friends feel for friends. Enjoy!

It is only the souls that do not love
that go empty in this world.
Robert Hugh Benson

We have all known loneliness, and we
have learned that the only solution
is love.

Dorothy Day

Friendship is a word the very sight
of which in print makes the heart warm.
Augustine Birrell

Friends are relatives
you make for yourself.

Eustache Deschamps

True friendship is
self-love at secondhand.
William Hazlitt

Love is not a state, it is a direction.
Simone Weil

Love can do all but raise the dead.
Emily Dickinson

Compassion is the chief law
of human existence.
Fyodor Dostoyevsky

We can do no great things;
   only small things with great love.
                    Mother Teresa

Love is, above all, the gift of oneself.
                    Jean Anouilh

Love is a multiplication.
Marjory Stoneman Douglas

Love is the essence of God.
Ralph Waldo Emerson

Friendship is in
loving rather than
being loved.

Robert Seymour Bridges

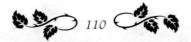

Best friend,
my wellspring
in the wilderness!

George Eliot

Thou shalt love thy neighbor as thyself.

Galatians 5:14

Sources

Sources

About the Author

Criswell Freeman is a Doctor of Clinical Psychology living in Nashville, Tennessee. In addition to this text, Dr. Freeman is also the author of many other books including his bestselling self help book *When Life Throws You a Curveball, Hit It.*

About
DELANEY STREET PRESS

DELANEY STREET PRESS publishes books designed to inspire and entertain readers of all ages. DELANEY STREET books are distributed by WALNUT GROVE PRESS. For more information, call 1-800-256-8584.